Ghetto Symphony:

Anthology of Zimbabwean Street Writing

Compiled and Edited by Mandhla A. Mavolwane

Typeset: Tendai R Mwanaka
Cover: **Streets of Chitungwiza- Ingwe Drive © Tendai R Mwanaka**

Mwanaka Media and Publishing Pvt Ltd,
Chitungwiza Zimbabwe

*

Creativity, Wisdom and Beauty

Publisher: Tendai R Mwanaka

Mwanaka Media and Publishing Pvt Ltd *(Mmap)*

24 Svosve Road, Zengeza 1

Chitungwiza Zimbabwe

mwanaka@yahoo.com

www.africanbookscollective.com/publishers/mwanaka-media-and-publishing

https://facebook.com/MwanakaMediaAndPublishing/

Distributed in and outside N. America by African Books Collective

orders@africanbookscollective.com

www.africanbookscollective.com

ISBN: 978-1-77906-508-7

EAN: 9781779065087

© Mandhla Mavolwane 2019

DISCLAIMER

iii

TABLE OF CONTENTS

About Editor

MANDHLA A. MAVOLWANE: Is an upcoming poet known as *The Psycho Poet* who writes to inform, enlighten and educate the masses on the pressing issues affecting our present reality and future tomorrow. The Psycho Poet is currently studying for an Undergraduate Honours Degree in Psychology at Midlands State University. In terms of his poetry work he is a contributor in the *Best New African Poets Anthology 2016, Africa, UK and Ireland: Writing Politics and Knowledge Production Volume 1* and *Zimbolicious Volume 3* and he intends to write his own books and continue to contribute his works in magazines and anthologies all around the world.

CONTRIBUTOR BIO NOTES

WILSON TINOTENDA WAISON: Born in 1998 being the first in a family of two. A son of Godwell Waison and Angeline Mandimaka (Electronic engineer and a manicurists) An ardent follower of the peace poetry association as well as the brains of Deem Literature organization. A protestant poet, human rights activist and a solidarity craftsman. Currently doing ACCA as a profession.

NORREST T. MANONGE: I am a Chegutu based young man aged 26 and a director of MNB COLLEGE, an academic institution. Also, a passionate writer whose origin is Buhera. Did Accounting, Economics and Business Studies at A level. I deferred my degree programme, Bachelor of Sciences honours degree in Agricultural Economics and Management...with Bindura Universiry of Science Education

CHANTELLE T. SEMU: is a lower six literature student at Glenview High. A public speaker as well as debater. Passionate about analysis and critical thinking. Writes poems and short stories. Ambition is to become a lawyer and part time author. Mainly focuses on the theme of women and poverty

TANIA CHIPO: I am a girl aged 18 currently doing my Lower Six at Zengeza 1 high school. I have always been interested in Art subjects and careers aligned to that. Being a poet particularly has always been my dream at a tender age. I'm mostly inspired by life experiences and in my recently written poem "My Intonation", daily societal situations actually drove me to write such a piece. The great desire in me is to become a profound author and also my role model

Mr Milton Kamwendo keeps encouraging me to advance in this poetic world.

COLLEN GAGA: Aka the *Dark Angel*, is a Protestant poet and a human rights activist. Born a Zimbabwean, and is the first from Gaga family. Currently a MSU Political science student doing his last year. He is the founding member of Ghetto diaries, and has many notable platforms he has performed in fine art.

BRIGHTON KAFIKAKO: I am an 18 year old Arts student at Zengeza 1 High School doing his Lower Sixth form. Mozambican by descent and Zimbabwean by birth, he is an aspiring Lawyer and a typist. Poetry became an obsession due to contact with Mrs. E Makwasha who is my mentor and Literature in English teacher. My family background also largely contributed to my work of art with the help of my mother Pamela Tarasika as my key motivator. My wish is to be the voice of the voiceless through my poetry and have true expressions of my feeling towards certain issues.

JANET GONDO: I was born on 3 November 1999 as the fourth born in a family of five in Chitungwiza. I am a public speaker and debater. My passion for words also saw me engaging in poetry and l desire to also partake in spoken word poetry. I started writing poems when l was in grade 5 after l realised that the words l had artistically arranged created a pleasing flow with a powerful message. Following this incident, l started writing more poems including Shona ones amongst them was one titled "Muti" (tree) in which I put myself in the life of a tree to deliver my message to the world and this won the *poem of the month* in the *Kwayedza Detembai Tinzwe 2011.* l desire to make meaningful noises on issues affecting the life of the child of this twenty first century through publishing my poems in various anthologies and probably write my own anthologies in my life time.

Introduction

The society is under bondages that are affecting the future of the current youth and young adult group. Such issues include child labour, child marriages, child prostitution, drug abuse and lack of entrepreneurship ideas to reduce poverty. The groups mostly affected by these challenges are under the education and small business sectors.

Minor school children are exposed to unduly and unfair child labour. Statistics from the last child labour survey (2011) concurred that about 10% of school children from the ages of 12-15 years are engaged in economic activities such as herding cattle, gardening and housekeeping duties because they live in low income families and in some cases they are orphaned. Hence such child labour activities can be fatal to physical health, mental health and educational capabilities.

In extreme cases these school children engage in child prostitution in order to make ends meet. Therefore child labour is a challenge to society as it harbours mental health illnesses, sexually transmitted diseases, impaired educational capabilities.

Child marriages and molestation affect today's young school students. Child marriages and child parenting are perpetrated towards the girl child usually by older adults or relatives. Young girls drop out of school to get married to older or same age groups as a supposed solution to poverty, child bearing and raising. Hence child marriages affect the education of the girl as she cannot acquire the good education that will help them in their future endeavours.

Negative peer pressure is one of the challenges responsible for the rapidly growing rate of drug abuse amongst the youth throughout Zimbabwe. The existence of inferiority complexes in all of us influences school children and young adults to want to be affiliated to a certain group of peers which can be their friends. Therefore such groups can be influential in negative ways and condone drug abuse behaviour thus influencing their other schoolmates. Zimbabwe's youth are an asset that will propel the country into the future so this asset must be safeguarded and guided on proper growth path to foster a change for the development of Zimbabwe and of the continent.

Lack of entrepreneurship ideas by young adults is crippling society. Education is there to train people for their tomorrow and to be able to conduct certain jobs that the subjects they studied prepared them for. Hence nowadays due to globalisation and technological advancement the world is constantly changing hence we have to adapt inorder to fit into the current socio-economic situations. Today's school students lack innovative ideas that will enhance and uplift their society, economy and people around them.

Therefore the *Ghetto Symphony* anthology is a blueprint guideline to a better tomorrow as it will highlight the factors affecting young adults and school students in Zimbabwe. Such factors include child labour, child prostitution, drug abuse and lack of innovative ideas as these are threatening Zimbabwe's tomorrow.

Fiction

STRAIN
Wilson Waison

I t was time...
   The dusk came, its greys swiftly risen and outstretched over the hamlets. Darkness reign yet to unleash its darker purpose of the readily dying day. Prospects deemed ... *KuMuvhu*ri. Proud slayers of decency imaged us though the quest of self sustenance. Six o'clock in winter, the sun readily fallen and the skies lit, moonlight......

   I got a quick rinse, warm bathe that creased off the ordours and a stint smell of the previous night. I felt the essence of being a human, afresh and glowing, I only wish it be the last thrive but hunger would claim more than a life. I got dressed, suited in my short silk shirt that revealed more than it could have concealed. My lips red smudged, hair nicely done and this fragrance ceasing breaths, attributing a trap for the brothers...

   Off I go *KuMuvhu*ri thinking aloud "*Nhasi handitambire zvichemo*, I need to cover my rentals and pick some groceries, I am out..." Each step I took drew me much closer of cemeteries, but what was left living for? Better was to embrace my early crafted death bed for life was a strain... What was worth living for? Just to die free or to live for a fee. The economic climate not so favorable and its burden harshly felt on my shoulders.

1

A five minute stroll from the cabins we all sort of call homes, I reached the work place. A local hot spot to be precise where all man from work pass by for a thrive before getting home to their families. Those with high rides, pedestrians and cyclists... I had no choice for all seemed resourceful to my plea. Their swollen pockets would answer to my solemn shout outs. With the cold, the cool breeze blowing, blizzards stinging alike an agitated swam of bees, adoption wasn't an option to this bad and harsh hazardous climatic condition. This business I had ventured into called for resilience.

Luckily as I stood forth for a chance, in no time came this young man, rolling wheels to where I stood, deemed his flash lights for the flash got me blared visions. I waved, smiling for no reason. He came closer and I knew it was all about the negotiations... Three years in the game, I had mastered the artistry of being a commercial sex worker. With the old memories that I dared not to recall... I blinked, for a moment I snapped and went off on a blackout...

Childhood, dad left when I was conceived
His gene did mold beauty, the beast now
Struggling for survival in the hamlet awry

A tatty retention that brought fears and shame to the family name, note that I had never known him who seized my mother's womanhood, he left, devoured *NeCheshuramatongo*. Mother was raped. She gave birth to a beautiful daughter before she died in theatre moments later... Granny told me I was seconds older and life revolved around grief and toil till I was fourteenth.

Puberty robbed me of my decency. I knew a man conjugally at Fifteen and the escapades distended my tummy, quick to realise I had

2

conceived, three months down the line it was not too late yet... It then marked my first abortion. Dropped school. Nearly died of the process for I had made a choice, not to raise a bastard whom I had no answers in case he would grow to know his biological father, whom I didn't know all my life I had lived to regret.

Eyes now wide open, I realised my visions as he drove close by... Could it be that I had been conscious? Moments past. He winded slowly his dark tinted window in a downward motion and blew a muted whistle. I stepped forth straight to converse,

"*Ndeyp!* Short time *imari nhasi*?" He bellowed

"Make it twenty *bamudiki*, You have it till we break backs" Face off his interior lighting,

"*Hapana mari wangu... ten ndinenge ndamira mira*" In a hesitant tone

"*Ita fifteen kwacho, uchafa nekuda zvemahara...*" I responded in a playful modus.

"Hop in *tichitaura, type yako ndochaiyo yaita nditize wepamba*"

We drove off to a local motel for the deeds. The room was so tense and scarlet lit, a sombre atmosphere masses in prevalence. Straight ahead I peeled off to skin readily waiting...He took off his shirt, left with a vest, undone his zipper ready for the easy dash.

The first penetration he had it on, a latex sheeting fitting the first round, pound upon pound him doing the going in and I doing the outing, out in and out. The second and third thriving became a mystery for he run out of latex. To me it was a take it or leave it, win win scenario as for so long I had been a walking grave, an ever fixed inheritance from my biological father. I had more to gain over losing...

Days past, Now that my rentals had been duly paid, I could lay low on market days and maximise proceeds off weekends. Friday

3

nights, readily booked for a dance show. A day before I had received a letter from the village which read...

Shupikai muzukuru, kuno hakuna chouviri, kubvira paya woenda dhorobha, hauzivi kuyeuka Dande. Kuno tapera nenzara kuda zvimwe runyoro rwangu rungakuyeuchidza kunobviwa iko woenda usiku...

My fiscal problems were just but a strain. I had equated life to a penis, easy contractions of gloomy penetrants. Back home granny was hunger stricken, dying of empty stomach, this added to my misery. How I wished things to have worked out in my favour.

Problems became reasons of my being.

GHETTO DIARY
Wilson Waison

Anew genesis spelt, with the rising dawn brought forth rinsed grandeur. Sited there, at the corner of the Bastille behind slabs. Impetuous thoughts in mind, waiting for the sixth hour mark for release, I felt the freedom. Then released.

Wondering how I ended up in that slammer, the odds had failed the math. It was on a regular Tuesday, busy than ever and I got lucky this time. I got away with it. Three days behind was just a hustle, *"tsoro dzangu ndangandabuda bobo..."*

Before I got busted early on, as of our normal drill we sited across the pavement and the tar bridge in jovial frame. The present atmosphere prevailing ceased breathes from the burst pipeline, sewage tickling off its main vent spilling onto the rough grounds, meandering off where we had the game on. Craze eight was not just a thing in the hoods, that's how we got jobbing proceeds to multiply before home reach.

"Kumaraini kwakazara ana mbavha..." Saint flow enchanting, *Ndo ghetto racho, "Ana mhamha vanorova anababa."* His song ridiculing the situation in our hamlets. The feminine voice was always on its highest pitch. Even the sisters where amidst us as we throw the dice, gambling. Gaming over the brothers, with one hand to the grounds, embracing my left footing, underneath laid a knife to counter resistance from the brothers.

Fortunes had my back. I triumphed over the local hustlers and swollen where my pockets, from the bounty. I picked a few groceries for mama at home. A bold lady I have ever known, who raised the brother and a sister in harmony and tranquil with the helping hand of the foster. Dad had been the backbone of the clan but gone were the days, as retrenchment got him booked off from the pay role. I had just turned fourteen and never knew these disparities of life and its illusions. Now that I was twenty, uncertain on the prospects tomorrow would hold for the brother, life testified a bitter sweet apple juice. Not so confined to take it as liquor or merely the fruit juice for it stood an ingredient of both calamities, sour brewery, red apple wine and at the other extreme apple hundred percent juice.

Such was life and its upbringings.

Went by the local supermarket. Reached home with heavy hands, mama puzzled. How...? I knew she was of unending questions, How I got the food stuffs was the first utterance from her sweetly pitched voice.

"Mom I got a big sale today," I lied in remorse, rebutting her lines.

"Rugare itange nhamo, Tsunga," she spoke in fury. I made no spoken reply, my head to the rhythmic phrase of hers, I nod. From the conversation I had readily been told, *"Rinamanyanga hariputire"* that shona proverb did not weird the matter at that minute. Moments later with the dusk approaching, darkness reigned in. Energies reverberated and the untold yet to unfold. Supper got me to the dining table, family moments. Tafadzwa my little sister spelt grace, holding hands. Delightful. I devoured in no time my served dish in a rush to go off...

Away from the hamlets, off we go. Signal fellow chaps off the streets down the railway line. Now that we had grouped, I being the mastermind of the plan in execution, poised two brothers as the eye, and the other three of us snapped across the wire fencing, stripped off the panelling and we found ourselves in, no alarm triggered. It was a smart dash. In a hurry brothers got hold of dark sacks, filled the bounty in 15 and off we go. Off the wall, skips and hop... All tricks worked out, just that I drew a blank on the surveillance, Chigwe got snapped. His capture by the camera got the whole pack endangered. Our escape was successful and the recovery was just but a misconception. Days past...

Splendid nights spent...In series of triumphs, as the dawn sparkle, the desires shift towards being straight. All answers to the call of duty, hustlers behind cabins in deep sleeps as daytime pose a hindrance to the mysterious profession. As darkness reign, the streets get heavy, with young sluts wondering for a chance to earn proceeds from the deeds, "*Ana sisi kumuvhuri*". On the other hand, as events unfolds, the brothers regrouping for another night shift. This time we had a hit on a local grocery store, forcefully find ourselves in the corridor, this was one of our greatest hit too. We had to hire a truck for our getaway. Lights deemed us from the rear, pushed the loaded van. Silently. Off the main street. It was clean like a whistle.

As of that day now, earlier on. I went for a drink with Chigwe, the other crew had to lay low for dusk to reign. Three quarters, I could feel the drowsiness... Minds raved off, brewage tasted bitter. With its soar sensation it brought out an elusive maze from all that I could gaze, a glimpse. Eyes itching, it was time I went off, head up I saw the brothers in blues and grey topped. In *nous* contemplations were of the bust, I narrowly escaped the cufflinks. Chigwe off guard got engulfed, cuffed and sent to the precinct slammer... Now that I was on the run, half a mile away I got relaxed. Unaware i had been recognised by an informant, he called Constable Chitanda Chimuti. In no time I was taken on the charges of public indecency,

The brother had been a sell-out.

7

I found myself to the corner of the slammer. I was an impotent detainee to the imaginary penitentiaries with the unleashed zeal to breakaway. That had been my providence, warped. Chromatics flared tinctures that shed a portal. A portray of misperception in my mind. Blues, reds, grey like in isolation revealing the concealed element so complex and ineptitude being my adversary an obstacle to that endeavor. A conclusion reached, it's a manifesto to the weak minds, daring for the goal to flee from the fancies, awake. It was merely elusive visions I had.

Two nights past, Mom worried, my whereabouts being her mystery. I couldn't lay heads, stings of fleas got me a rinsed agitation, Pulex irritants. Locked in. Behind Slabs. The graffiti of former apprehends raving minds a milestone, its vivid portrayal fostering that bandit vibe. I had never felt fear like that. Defiant knowingly the courts had my back. As I embraced the feeling felt, this other brother in blues and grey tops came and bellowed aloud, Nhamo, Tonderai and Gari out we head to court for justice. Coincidence, Chigwe had been scheduled for the same date. Eyed him in fury. He went in first and got a light sentence for the clan, three months behind for breaking in was not a hustle. In, still apprehended...

Facing the jury, held the bible for honest responses, shivering. I shacked off the fears. A second glance at the jury I gained my lost confidence. Reminiscing the statement I had made before, held on charges of indecency, potential suspect of a factory burglary and assault of the two officers who had me behind bars. Those were pretty much the counts to my name, broadly a first time offender I thought... was I really? Interrogation commenced and I triumphed over the prosecution, trickster as had been of my profession. Got my

Three hundred hours of community service, to be performed in seven hours of each market day.

THE MILL
Wilson Waison

Old... pacing towards the corner store, like a toddler, crawling straight to the Mill. Skinny, she resembled a scare crawl amid the maize stalks, blown left right. She got to the stoep, put down the sack and found herself a sit before the stoep. The sack was half-filled in a grey packing bag, grains bored. Insect infested I protested in a pail muted voice pouring the remains of it in the mill for grinding...

Heads down to pick forth two more sacks thrown. Bending harshly, breaking backs to the weight of the muddling fiscal burdens. Busy than ever as has been the peak of the day, dusk in descending. Darkness yet to reign and that reddish ray outstretched to the outskirts of the hamlets. We waved off one more day of misery to the discordant sound of the mill which inflicted much trauma, eardrums bursting fails the dead silence of the winters. And a cold air mass in prevalence as barren as the winter itself.

Survival pointed to the fittest bull, as in streets brothers were in rage, due to... due to... Devoid of anyone sagacious, they pledged beast upon beast, horn to horn in ramps of revulsion's peak all in response to the rinsed slogans and chants. As if not, that had been the system for decades, each polling claimed a fellar. Brothers dropped dead if they do not render their compliance. I am of this sentiment, veto always had the vote.

Prejudice and tendentiousness had become an integral part of the societies, those with influence were most feared, peasantry bred to grow butter for their porridge's enrichment. Only a normal life could cherish what they broadcast on the local station. Escaping into their world we all longed to reach. Poverty got us sandals to school, slopes or even barefoot, we trod for the forthcoming salvation.

Contrary to the rampages, sisters in harmony, busy bees in collection of nectar, pollen stick fertilizing our colorful petal like traditions, romanticizing our ethics and strain morality. Busy ants in built of a new citadel spelt of virtue from a range, shame cast for transactional sex, no more a vice. Exploited for the bond in circulation, if not bondage. Performing for a token of appreciation in return, Oh! What a dying day it turned be... Future prospective blared as mothers foster barbaric acts yet fathers turns to be the witnesses of such immoral acts... Muted.

In three, her maize poured off pipes, mealie milled of a dusty white fine granules black spotted, I dared not even a glimpse. Hocked off the grey sack side facing, received the bond note offered at displeasure. In return I changed her with plenty brown coins, that torn pockets if not carefully placed. Not to mention, inflation rates that had readily loomed to a twenty five percent mark, fiscal dilemmas carried with it, the notes. A new misperception in the masses' perception, no emancipation rendered by being ruled with a scepter, totalitarian chiefs in my home town.

We made a couple of grinds before closing. Shacked off the dust. Heads white. At ease I found myself in the bathe for a rinse. My peel sensational to the bathe, creasing off the ordure dirt...

11

NATASHA

Wilson Waison

Even the rising dawn had brought a curse, we longed for better prospects from her... She was so bright, with good grades each team.

Mainini had bored her at tender phases of life. Fifteen was just too much to be a child bearer. She was so young and she raised her in remorse but she decided to partake the same fate. She could see her behind closed doors being molested, all that pain and agony she never learnt from.

Sitted. Sun busking and its scorching ray sensational to the peel, Drawn in deep thoughts of the boy responsible for impregnating her, my wrath did grew. Both from the burns and memories unfolding that moment. I readily had been paranoid.

A school leaver, hustler at a local pub, Mashabhini, a lowlife just like the rest in the hood ... How could she possibly had fallen for such a feign. All these impetuous thoughts brought about shame to the family name.

It was time she went off to her matrimonial home...

Previously as a concerned brother I had asked her about the deeds and she denied all allegations I laid on her. Later the truth came to pass. Long deceitful wiles had been posed, even Mainini couldn't tell who to blame was my quest.

This other night, in a jovial frame at the pub came a close mate. Drinks on me, spoiling the brother in crime. We drank our souls out, and that was the thanks I got, Tsano *vako* made a big sale today. *Hanzvadzi yako haicheme Mfesi akatokabira arikutsvaga den* to lay heads, he burst into a laughter, In nous I was puzzled and it made no sense, subconsciously meditating on that phrase, on my way home. It weird no matter that moment.

Got home, two of my little sisters in a deep sleep. Went straight to my spare restroom and dozed off... Snoring heavily, puffing out thick air, that sting, off sheets. Sweating, dripping wet. Hot summer nights, mosquito infested stinging and sapping off my veins, pulse faintly felt.

***

Listening attentively to one of Charles Charamba's great hit entitled, *Muchazoveiko vana vangu vevamwe vanodadisa* It ironically posed these questions I had no clues to offer.

"*Ndidzo dzakaita mukurumbira tichakura*", Baba said.

Deeply tracking the message being heralded, Natasha bellowed "*I will bring forth wonders*", Baba paying particular attention. I ignored the small talk...

"*Vanangu hupenyu mutoro, dzidzo inhaka youpenyu*", Baba responded as I nodded to the tranquil orchestra from the song. It pitched perfectly the ghetto symphony, its restrictions and problematic issues it brought about. For moments, we seemed be on the same page, striving to attain a better life. That is the call we all seemed to have been answering .

The conversation got deep, neither was I paying particular attention. I had been staring at the news feeds which heralded;

Zimbabwe is open for business, as had been the joke of the day...
The ease of doing business, political motivated statements...
Corporate Zimbabwe in conjunction with the SMEs...

13

That had been the Economic forum show, the presenters walking the talk. With the economic downturn being faced by masses, it raved my mind a milestone. In deep thoughts, implementation was not just a problem but the root cause to the damaged economic ecosystem. Unemployment rates had never dropped a hundredth. Corruption and Nepotism had been the hustle, in the fiscal sector the bond in circulation. Exchange rates reaching a climax of more than twenty five percent. Bank lines cutting across main streets, people waiting, patiently to receive not more than a tenth of their salaries. Just the thought of it sapped all my energies for so long I had also been a victim of the prevalent circumstances.

Innovation had been a misfit. The dilapidated scenery of our cribs had also been a pivot in breeding proud ethic monsters, in streets proud mobsters and shameless gangsters. Sanity had proved a tough math as garbage was barely collected, maybe once every fortnight and reasons never told since we had been paying off dues in time. Municipalities had been stagnant, having a shortfall on vital services yet to be delivered. Poor water provision left the street of Chitungwiza with countless wells as if it was conducive, half a metre away from a septic tank for toilet refuse.

Days past. On a Wednesday night, it was about time we had supper. Natasha had prepared the dish, surprisingly she had onion off her menu. We ate at displeasure. No one ever said a word nor raised a concern. It became her routine. She would buy dried *masau*, ate more than usual, that rose alarms. She had completely changed her diet. I noticed, she became too weary for her daily chores and would sleep long hours than she would normally do. You would find her in a deep sleep during day hours, but it never got my mind a corkscrew. I had been relaxed to her sudden changes, after all I had been nothing but a distant cousin. She had a stance in her speech and her actions proved her defiance, she was rude.

***

Family moments became a thing and we would all eat at once, however she had lame excuses off the dinner table. It had become a habit. She was now skipping school for petty reasons. Today it's her backside giving her a strain, the day after she got a headache, on and on. We all had got used to her excuses. All those excuses were wonders manifesting, I questioned my conscience.

A month passes, rare developments being noticed now. Mama was now concerned about her flow, she had skipped a cycle. Biology proved it normal due to, due to... Other young women have been diagnosed with a familiar problem. It was even made a National concern, Blood clot in cervix due to, due to... cervical issues had left many in disparity. A common cancerous symptom she claimed that had been her case too. Mama got worried, she took her for a medical check. Nothing of that sort was spelt, the doctors were positive.

And then approached the dusk. Mother readily knew. Baba and us were in suspense, so concerned with her condition, for we thought of the devouring cervical cancer. However, the screens proved us wrong. It called for a relief though the other side of the story wasn't yet spelt. Neither of the them had a better stance, Natasha in tears. It made no sense maybe it had been of joy when she realised she had no cancer of that sort. Mama called us all for a moment, I thought

15

that was just about her negative results. Eager to acknowledge what she had to say, I was the first in response to her call out.

Natasha was diagnosed negative, it's not cancer however she might have seen a man. I could tell, Baba was troubled... I thought of the thanks I had earlier received at the pub, Mashabhini. It's all weird the matter, and I got her to converse

"Is it not what I am thinking, Its Rufaro, is it not?"
"No." How lame she denied,
"Are you pregnant chisikana?" Baba asked angrily

"I am not", she protested. All family members got nervous and went off to bed. I continued with the interrogation, she replied "stop with the allegations and accusations".

HIDDEN TREASURE
Norrest Tinashe Manonge

Even in that ancient Dzimbabwe, you would contemptibly
live as a girl

Neglected, labelled, belittled and rejected like a louse, you
lived hidden

in a dustbin rolling in a dust cart in a dust bowl yet you are
a treasure.

Even 1980, the freedom foundation, found you missing in
the family love.

Jarred and marred, enslaved, charred, rapped and messed
minus support,

you would despicably live a treasure trove; an open secret
of life we must conserve

In bigoted and bedevilled present societies where there is
no girl to conserve,

you live suppressed, but a boy lives to be groomed. We regret; sorry girl!

A boy learns to live and you, our girl, live to learn about life void of support

Stratified; a boy carries no duty, but a girl-all chores plus other hidden,

strenuous and demotivating tasks. Bliss for a boy and blisters for the treasure!

Girl boy- new oxymoron; girl=oxus (dull); boy=moros(sharp). God forbid! Give us love

All had been millions of nauseating prejudices. We are sorry. Yet you can direly love.

And between Nehemiah and Job boldly stood Esther! That's the girl's grit to conserve.

A girl child is not a treasury bill; she is a treasury bond; an interest bearing treasure.

Ruth is standing between wise Judges and King Samuel! Rise today and shine our girl.

She adds to the nation; give her chances. Prise out this evil omen that's aloof hidden.

A girl conceives her knowledge and her kings; to Jesus, Mary gave a plausible support.

A girl lives our benevolent and focused Mother Theresa who dared to support

We would despise you a girl child, we deserve penalties, absolve us and pour love

Flattered and buttered by detractors we battered...and ruined you...we're guilt; we kept you hidden

We are a nation, caste and family to blame; for your better, our treasure, we flop to conserve

Enthralled and veiled by our myopias, we lost you the key to success, the pretty girl

 Masters and ministers where are you? Repent by endowing a girl child, our treasure Even in that ancient *Dzimbabwe, you* would contemptibly live as a **girl**

Neglected, labelled, belittled and rejected like a louse, you lived **hidden**

in a dustbin rolling in a dust cart in a dust bowl yet you are a **treasure.**

Even 1980, the freedom foundation, found you missing in the family **love.**

Jarred and marred, enslaved, charred, rapped and messed minus **support,**

you would despicably live a treasure trove; an open secret of life we must **conserve**

In bigoted and bedevilled present societies where there is no girl to **conserve,**

you live suppressed, but a boy lives to be groomed. We regret; sorry **girl!**

A boy learns to live and you, our girl, live to learn about life void of **support**

Stratified; a boy carries no duty, but a girl-all chores plus other **hidden,**

strenuous and demotivating tasks. Bliss for a boy and blisters for the **treasure!**

Girl boy- new oxymoron; girl=*oxus* (dull);
boy=*moros*(sharp*)*. God forbid! Give us **love**

All had been millions of nauseating prejudices. We are
sorry. Yet you can direly **love.**

And between Nehemiah and Job boldly stood Esther! That's the
girl's grit to **conserve.**

A girl child is not a treasury bill; she is a treasury bond; an
interest bearing **treasure.**

Ruth is standing between wise Judges and King Samuel! Rise today
and shine our **girl.**

She adds to the nation; give her chances. Prise out this evil
omen that's aloof **hidden.**

A girl conceives her knowledge and her kings*; to Jesus,
Mary gave a plausible* **support.**

A girl lives our benevolent and focused *Mother Theresa* who dared to **support**

We would despise you a girl child, we deserve penalties, absolve us and pour **love**

Flattered and buttered by detractors we battered…and ruined you…we're guilt; we kept you **hidden**

We are a nation, caste and family to blame; for your better, our treasure, we flop to **conserve**

Enthralled and veiled by our myopias, we lost you the key to success, the pretty **girl**

Masters and ministers where are you? Repent by endowing a girl child, our **treasure**

THE UNFRIENDLY NIGHT
Shantel Semu

I watch her as she changes
Into her usual skimpy clothes
A peck on the cheek
And she is swallowed by the night
My mother
A lady of the night

Yet another lonely night
A faint creak of the rusty gate
Hushed voices
Rushed footsteps
Tall male figures appear
From the eerie silence of the night
Slammed doors and muffled screams
My innocence was stolen by the night

Six months pregnant
I lie still in the unfriendly night
Loud singing from a drunkard
Music blasting from the nearby beerhall
Dogs barking, piercing whistles
And I wonder who is going to be the victim tonight

Eighteen years later
I watch him getting ready
To go and torment poor souls

Armed with a mask and knife
My fatherless son
Disappears into the unfriendly night

NO PLACE FOR A CHILD
Shantel Semu

A thick layer of dust covers the sky
As bare footed children run around
My heart yearns to join them
But mother will not hear of it
As she says
The streets are no place for a child

A group of boys are huddled in a corner
School dropouts they are
From the distance I cannot see what
But I know they are sniffing something
Wish their parents had told them
That the streets are no place for a child

Here is Rudo passing by
Fifteen and pregnant
Eyes lowered in an attempt to hide
From the prying eyes of gossiping women
And jeers from playing children
I understand that indeed
The streets are no place for a child

A small crowd has started to gather
Peter and his wife are at it again
Tearing each other's clothes away
Yelling all sorts of obscenities

Mother silently escorts me into the house
Muttering under her breath
The streets are no place for a child

MY INTONATION
Tania Chipo

Family!
The thought flickered through my mind,
I had to start my own family.
With the so-called good-for-nothing scum
I had to build my own home for there was nothing remarkable left of
me,
Vapid and tasteless, my life had become.
Indeed I was swept of all my pride
And this is my intonation.

Mom and dad had all kicked the bucket,
Without a proper valediction they departed,
For sure they were to return no more.
Relatives forgot while friends forsook me,
Gradually life began to lose flavour,
It became meaningless as I was then hopeless.
A great sadness gripped my chest,
Like a hot and tight iron band it jabbed me.
At only sixteen I was to bear the weight of the world
Upon my shoulders, so I gave in
Yes I gave in to his proposal.

School?
What worth did it still hold to me?
After failing so dismally I gave up.
The thought of the unpaid school fees

And the successive failure experiences
Squashed off all my strength to persevere.
And so I had to give it a halt.

As a girl child what else was I supposed to do?
Absolutely nothing.
With such a picky background
And a life with variegated experiences,
I sensed my life drawing to cessation.
I had to be married
And here I am now,
A nursing infant.
My intonation.

NEW ERA OR NEW ERROR
Tania Chipo

They all applauded in happiness
As they welcomed the drastic change.
It marked the beginning a new crisp chapter,
For the order of the things had actually changed.
It saw a transition in manners and way of operation
And they called it the start of a new era.
But was this really a new era or it was a new error?

Its encroachment opened the eyes of the natives,
They became xenocentric.
For the love of foreign goods,
They discarded their cultures and values,
Replacing their once modest dressing
With an indecent one.
Sacredness once lay in a woman's thighs
But now modest apparel is linked with poverty, women now apply
clothing instead of wearing.
And you call that new era?

Promiscuity and prostitution
Seem to be the world's top business.
Girls breaking their virginity for a two-dollar note.
Whilst men and women abandon their families
Only in the name of pleasure.
Nollywood and Hollywood fans, they claim to be .
New era, or New error?

If you can't own then steal,
I have heard my uneducated brothers talking.
But is this really how things are supposed to be?
Ethical conducted has been corrupted,
European concepts have been Africanized
But alas! They failed to produce the identical thing.
They did in acting and we've taken it for daily life.
It maintained their worldviews
But it has corrupted our virtues.
Fellow brethren is this still the new era thing?

I can't get it all.
I tried not to give my own definition.
I think I need to take a closer look,
For I might be having a myopic vision.
What's the correct term fellow Zimbabweans
New era or New error?

VANITY
Wilson Waison

The trait of being vain and conceited
Hast took odds in the domains, vanities , vanity
Mirrors to reframe my posture, a man behind
Weild decency in defence of his faults, faulty

The domain an incubator of ills, shame cast
Immunity all spoke of self- righteousness too
Egocentric spawn schemes vile, shame cast
To apprehend the brother and devoid too

Revulsions parades daily, now our norms
And that sensation to gaze away impedes
Even father is involved, only to provide arms
To further fragment the ethos, and stampedes

Mother and sisters brawls for their rights
Reserved then only to perform conjugally
For not more than a dollar note, Vile outs
Shame cast, ethnic monsters bred proudly

Vanity vines piles, a new castle erected
Confusing though the verge at play strange
Taboos performed, Incestuous, Morality ejected
To elect this page, printed virtuous from a range.

BLACK-ISM
Wilson Waison

Even hen vulture nurse her eggs up high
Reasons, man is not to be trusted easily
How hen eagle is keen to table her cries
Folly is "us" humane wrathful we can be
To destroy what we intend not to build...

Savage brother lure me into submission
Lashed and stroked too, backs breaking
Dehumanized, those with the mighty to
Foster punitive conditions alike Warsaw
Ghettoized by blood, vulture's prey turns

Dropping dead alike roses in arid soils
Sapped thy waters of life's sustenance
Wilts to the harsh radiant beams of the
Sun yet too it's a necessity for thy grow
How will we mature to our full potential?

Poised betwixt many crowns, delusions
Told of illusory ideas that will propel us
Jinxed in those memo of tatty retention
Colonial impediments no longer offend
For man crafted many *isms*, stampede.

STRAIN
Wilson Waison

Childhood, dad left when I was conceived
His gene did mould beauty, the beast now
Struggling for survival in the hamlet awry
Gambling, hustling conjugal visits for not
More than a dollar note. Some to blame me
For these deeds but my reasons never told
Confused on what to call it though the quest
Points to survival in this economic depression.

Some scores, mocks and take me for a joke
Even my conscience is painted black perceived
To be a villain not the victim how absurd it is
On my verge a victim of circumstances, how
Beautiful. I pay the bill and some dues from
Revulsion sacred bounty yet still names I am
Called, Harsh and cold hearted are my sisters
And brothers not concerned about my affair.

LAB RAT
Wilson Waison

Bred for pranks and known too many
Fancies from the dosage, syringe hurt
Cold nights endured for their dictates..
Warmth so rinsed in our nudity covers
Courage no longer a remedy healing us

Calamitous experience now normalized
Yet too the discordant drummer still
Pounds and us to dance even in denial
For fate has got the brother ghettoized
And Warsaw deeds practiced by Forster

Innocent souls claimed, brute force to
Disperse us in cages, our reaction too
Termed protests. Voicing concern to be
Liberated and November turned a black
Christmas, July preceding August slain

The impetuous sisters got inseminated
More lab rats bred for their dictates awry
Less and less immune induced to count
And her milk dries from the heats, poor
Administration cost us lives at the mall.

STREET BULLETIN
Wilson Waison

Across the bridge, where we lay heads
Is our foster's corpse with drained lung
And tears no longer ooze for the deeds
Are now a pragmatic norm,sister perish
Too, from sex slavery upon a parturition

And our numbers increasing every day
Abandoned, rejected, segregated yet too
We have grown to be outcasts, socially
Excluded by the society surrounding us
Termed unpleasantly, Street children...

How the bird tweet irritates every dawn
Acknowledging a bitter day ahead of us
Dehumanized by those with homes too
Left vulnerable to these exploitative airs
That I labour for a pinch of sugar for tea

From the fields we fail the weeds for no
Return maybe one or two corn to roast
Tummies hunger inflamed and the soft
Intestinal walling torn down, ulceration
Inflicting more painful sorrows. In street

SKUNK
Wilson Waison

I found my brains melting and oozing
From my ears after strokes, the spiffs
And the aftermath were way too fatal
Brainstorming to these rinsed grandeur
I felt this strength with a nerve to bite
Teething heavily, I escaped into fancies

Being a billionaire at tender phases of
Life, hyperinflated currency that swells
All my pockets. Buying bread cost more
Of a fortune and oil being rationed too
Gambling for survival playing ourselves
Alike a solitaire, bidding unreasonably.

And now the drips getting heavy, ousted
Emptying my skull, a mad man's crafted
Impetuous contemplations. Realities be
Calamitous in this economic shipwreck
And the waves so heavy to fail all these
Instruments engaged as of the solution

More strokes from the spiff gasping air
Smoke frost conscience shading darkies
Future held in the palm of savage paint
Blared canvas of historical ethos, pains
Many wars being fought in minds awry

Skunk, skunk's stings and left half dead

FEAR
Wilson Waison

Raised in harmony and tranquillity, from infancy
Never was I poised between these storms that's
Disillusionment and Disparity, tolls in prevalence
Childhood being and been a bliss, gone by blasts

Hell on earth is the odds, a sour bite of truths
So savage and raves the minds a milestone away
Escapism votes my fate through veto, sad thoughts
Derived each second of this phase of livelihood.

Once the brave diva that raised an innocent son
Descendant to the wise crown, tore apart the tires
Readily a nob that had been strained and fragile
To have pulled the string all will point vehemently.

What shall it became this lifeless experience cast
Fist upon fist, pound of flesh bled... oozes blood
Stained be the cordial relation strained due to...
Due to... These episodes brought about my fears.

TILL DARKNESS PREVAIL

Wilson Waison

With which rising dawn do I see good?
Nor bad to denote with the demise too
Poised betwixt two crowns "virtue-vice"
Held on prejudice, yet I know not sanity

Mother told she went overseas for job
Seeking, far away across the boarders
Beyond the highs of Inyangani, faraway
Told the economies held responsible...

Father never known him from infancy
Told he denied this sexual escapades
Raised as of a base bastard by foster
Sire, to know more of wrathful speeches

Till darkness prevail I know not sanity
Grandma dry jokes fail my laughter yet
She wipes out the sacred waters off eyes
Shedding tears being more of a hobby...

Her shoulder getting heavier as she ages
More lifeless experiences too for I have been
Depending, now tables to have turned...
Aged and weary, she looks up to me too

DAILY STRUGGLES
Wilson Waison

Life staged into a war zone of conflicting
Morals, passions and reasons never cleared
And I burst out aloud a cry in vain for none
Hast yet heard or ever felt for the brother...

Some even take tolls and judge my low
Lived existence of a grasshopper leaping
Into the visage of danger, stereotyped and
A victim of circumstances too, lowlife diarist.

Prayer points for a better day to reign
Terror inflicts no pains anymore, only gains
My crafted death bed glimmer more than
My jewel, nor wonder the French man thought.

Is it not fate to die by the gun if life ever turns?
Revolves around massacres of decent and
Innocent souls, bred to know more about death
Than about living. Daily struggles in the domain

HOME SWEET HELL

Collen Gaga

"I paid my money to bring you here'
I own you, you belong to me!"
He screams every night at the apex of his voice. Hearing his voice
In the yard signals trouble.
I have to hide the girls.
Too bad I was not whole when he knew me
But he did not bother then, now
Even the fruits of his waist he doubts their paternity.
He is the beer hall himself, stinky breath
Barking in my face.
Peace is long gone run away and escaped from my heart and soul.
The brew is always yelling, pushing and hitting.
"Where are those illegitimates?"
Throw them out of my house they go find their father
Their mother is a harlot, she is here for my money
I know right, well I need conjugal equivalencies.
He groans like a hurt monster and pushes me to the mat
"Lie down and let me enjoy my cattle before you kill me
Your poor father gave you to me because he needed my wealth like
you do"
Helplessly I lay as he torture the essence of my memories.
My fragmented heart repeatedly broadcast horror stories that thrill
my emotions
Asking who will rescue me?

RIPPED CORAZON
Brighton Kafikako

Sleepless nights...
Tiresome days...
Tell me, is this what you need to feel better?
I know you mistake this other guy for the Cupid.

My tears drip like sweat...
Is this how you act when you know we are forever?
But you can come back whenever?
I am not Romeo...
I would rather take a life for you.

From sweet day dreams...
I see you in my nightmares.
At least scold me when I call you
Because your silence imbrues my love.

A soporific cannot induce sleep in me
Your love might be the sedative.
I'm just wandering in the desert of love...
I'm thirsty, your presence might be the oasis.

BROKEN MIRROR
Mandhla Mavolwane

The retina opens the doorway to the subconscious
A doorway to no man's land
Panorama surrounding is jinxed.
Who conceived the bastard insecurity?
A bastard breastfed with anxiety
The only nourishment after weaning was tasteless esteem.

The sour taste saliva is betrayal swallowed
Crooked teeth formed by lies and deceit.
The tongue stain is a patch of broken relationships
Pink-black lips burnt by immoral kisses.

Echoes of the eardrum are mixed signals.
Appraisal of successes are inadequate,
Curses and insults evoke trust issues,
Lectures have a hate speech rhythm,
Loud headphone music inspires hard work.
Pardon the damaged eardrums' misinterpretation of conversations.

I put the mirror down,
And wonder what it could reveal
If it wasn't broken.

THE JUDAS KISS
Mandhla Mavolwane

To have known you in my teenagehood
Ours was love at first sight
You were seductive when dripping cold sweat,
You were sweet when ice cold.
A sip of you gave cold butterfly sensations.
I swear you were a truth serum,
You gave life to fantasies like Walt Disney,
What more could a fool desire?

"Hell hath no fury like a woman scorned"
I found the meaning when you were warm
A sip of you tasted like crocodile bile,
Bile so intoxicating I puked my thorax out.
Lustful desires urged me to forgive you
As I learnt only to devour you dripping cold sweat.

My love for you pains deeper than the wound inflicted by Cupid's
arrow.
The cold sensations made me speak profane truths.
The fantasy bubble burst up
My reality was chronic headaches.
Today a glimpse of you is nauseating.
Like Antonio, I sacrificed my pound of flesh,
And today dialysis is my new lover,
Whom I tell about your Judas kisses.

43

THE EPIPHANY
Mandhla Mavolwane

An enigmatic voice faintly echoes
"Mental impairment and chronic disorders are the side effects"
Episodes of paranoia about the inevitable future?
Anxiety about how will i say out my name?
To strangers who also succumbed to the same fate of dependency on
narcotics.

The tree of life is endangered
As its forbidden fruit is now on auction
The buyers are chauvinists only seeking pleasure
Economic instability has doomed us all
As the tree of life is succumbing to deforestation
In a bid to obtain nurturing nutrients.

Society has changed into a dreadful place.
Like a tsunami it has gobbled up
Innocent maidens and damsels.
Turning them into property and artifacts.
What has become of this spiteful society?

Deep meditation absorbs the tragedy
And an inquisitive tone utters
"Are you proud of this unruly mess?"
A question piercing to the core of the heart and mind
What then is the answer?

Waking up from slumber and mental inertia
Developing an allergy to opiates and stimulants.
Engaging in proper ways of earning income
Eradicating prostitution and crime.
Crimes against the feminine should be checked.

An ecstatic frenzy kicks in
As the epiphany unfolds.

THE NOVEMBER CHRISTMAS
Mandhla Mavolwane

Known to come once a year,
Santa made some drastic changes!
Ecstatic behaviour was the joy of all
The old jinx had been dismantled
And we experienced a double Christmas

Little did we know about opposing nature
We are now facing the wrath of nature.
First it was contaminated water and food.
Life subdued on a toilet seat.
To save life we had to compromise,
A shortage of commodities was the counter-attack.

The outcry against digital money finally heard
Now the green paper is overflowing.
People in long frustrating queues are liberated
As they now queue with entertainment in their cars.
Will they introduce plastic fuel?

Christmas came twice in a year.
Jingle bells are exiled this year.
We gormandized all the food last November,
We exhausted all the fuel last November,
We were all healthy last November,
This year's Christmas was last November!

GHETTO SYMPHONY
Mandhla Mavolwane

Wandering helplessly under the scorching sun
How did we get here?
Discord rhythms of hunger pangs drove us to this intoxicating
wasteland.
Like Rhode's grave inscription
Here lies the remains of excavated gems
Gems that will subdue starvation.
Instead of fighting the indigence around us
The wound is deepened by greed.

Under the watch of the night sky
The streets have witnessed all of it.
Only a flash of headlights signal interest.
After dawn the previous spark has vanished.
Chronic ailments reunite the young slut and lustful jerk.
The streets have devoured the decency of people

The matrimonial contract is now invalid
As everyone has turned a blind eye
In overseeing the rightful age of
Signing the sacred contract.
Mayhem and barbaric acts are end products of the wedlock
vulnerable damsels.
Will the witnesses of such immoral acts pluck out these habits.

Like Boxer in the legendary Animal farm
We work to end the turmoil threatening a better tomorrow.
A tomorrow that is free from ailments,
Invalid matrimonial contracts and
Streets that only know legitimate professions.

NOREEN
Mandhla Mavolwane

Efforts to weep were unfruitful
I held in my tears like a fart.
The lump in my throat still chokes me.
I will use ink to mourn your innocence,
I will use paper to describe your potential.

Childhood games today seem like dèjà vu,
You are now a mother to a son,
But it pains me that you dropped out of school.
It's a nightmare that you're a statistic.
Statistic of young pregnant damsels.

Childhood flashbacks are mere fantasies.
You mastered A,B,C like a wiz
While I struggled to get past B.
Jealousy and envy faked my congratulations speech.
Teenage pregnancy evaporated all that potential.

Dreams and aspirations vanished like morning dew,
But it is never too late to make amends.
You mistakenly defied societal norms
And now it's time to dismantle societal stereotypes.
Resurrect the burning fire to succeed
Then I will finally weep tears of joy.

CROOKED SMILE
Mandhla Mavolwane

A dark cloud hovers over juveniles.
Instead of defining a balanced diet,
Primary pupils define massive unemployment.
Zebra crosses are now an ancient road sign,
Whilst potholes are the new age road signs
What kind of knowledge is power?

Under the watch of the scorching sun,
Recital of pledges like spoken word poetry.
The August mayhem queries the daily recital.
Like a diabetes wound, its failing to heal.
Which version of patriotism will brainwash them?

The diarist scribbled affluence to all.
The low-life have to survive to be fit.
The psychos have to be fit to survive.
Frequent exercise reduces their cholesterol prescriptions,
Salt and sugar solution reduces our dehydration.
How will you explain ailments under social class?

United we have suffered immensely.
Freedom after speech is a bet placed at Africa bet.
Like Jacob we long to devour the fruits of our labour.
The hoe no longer guarantees bumper harvests
And the rifle has gone rogue.
When will they comprehend the arms coating our existence?

The monuments testify our colourful culture,
The fertile soil and precious gems symbolize our wealth.
The education civilised our livelihood.
Why are we cursed with crooked smiles?

REFLECTIONS
Mandhla Mavolwane

The winter breeze is polluted.
Polluted by a stench of indigence
Entrepreneurship has been misinterpreted
During daytime they are vendors
But the moon knows them as harlots and thieves.
Are those the effective weapons to fight poverty?

A remnant flower is growing
As it is being watered by tears.
Tears of an oppressed maiden
Bound by marital duties to a senile cur.
Reduced to a mere sexual object
Only the flower knows her plight.

A futile philosophy numbs the mind
Physical and mental fatigue are the visible traits.
Traits of the exploitation of vibrant juveniles.
Can a calf put on a yoke grow into a strong bull?

The catch them young philosophy is destructive
As juveniles are slowly self-destructing.

Like Christ this society has to resurrect from the dead
Resurrect with innovation to combat poverty,
Emancipation from the shackles of unlawful marriages
And bear reflections of a fruitful societal structure.

DEAR ANXIETY
Mandhla Mavolwane

Dear anxiety,
Today I devour breakfast with superstition,
I quench my thirst with paranoid thoughts.
Street bulletins report hazards in nourishment food.
Seeking refuge under fasting is inevitable.
Hunger pangs will gladly deliver me to starvation.

Dear anxiety,
I read about breath taking graduation ceremonies,
The next page headlines violent jobless protesters.
I question the enigmatic purpose of acquiring knowledge,
If jobless graduates are an inflated currency.

Dear anxiety,
The breadwinner burden crash landed on my shoulders.
Father disappeared like King Lobengula,
Ailments confined mother to her poverty stained bed,
Little sister dreams of being an accountant.
Street hustling is the high paying profession.

Dear anxiety,
Daily publications echo squeler's utterances
Self-sufficiency is the persuasive assurance,
Yet the naked eye espies deficiency.
Panic is the word on the street,
State of affairs are loosening the Napoleonic grip.

Dear anxiety,
Will I survive this quicksand environment?

NARCOTIC LOVE
Mandhla Mavolwane

I feel numb,
Everything is a deadlock
The reminiscing gear is on
What happened? How did
I end up in this state?
Oh yes! My lover devoured
The life out of me.
How could she mislead me!
I burnt my lungs for her
I wasted my liver for her
I damaged my brain for her
And today I am a corpse.
She is still out there
With new lovers
Enticing them with her
Intoxicating narcotic love.

DECEIVED
Janet Gondo

The promise came on a silver platter
Too good to resist.
Mesmerised was i at the sight of it
Tantalising was the smell to my noise
A mouth-watering sensation it was,
But little did i know that behind the white smile of this
generous Moses who had promised me a free and joyful Canaan
Was a menacing cavity that was slowly corroding her teeth.

Yes i accept that i was a fool to believe that this woman would be
Kind enough to send me to school
A promise to my poverty stricken parents!
Today i fail to comprehend why I'm sold
For sexual pleasures.
I thought she pitied my suffering
I thought her intentions were clear and clean,
Obviously i had thought wrong.
She isn't the generous Mother Theresa
To wipe away the tears of suffering children
But she is a girl trafficker

At her service, many girl children have been sexually exploited.
Feeding off their innocence for breakfast
Their suffering for lunch
And for dinner she violates their right to be protected
from exploitative labour practices.

Girl child tears and blood fuels her cars as she drives
To deceive other girls so that her brothel grows.

Beware my fellow girl children
Women have become enemies of themselves,
Girl trafficking is no longer a man's profession.
If the promises you receive from a helper appear too good
Know that they cannot be true.

DAYLIGHT ROBBERY
Janet Gondo

My Lord
Today on trial i bring you
   the greatest criminal offence
   ever to be created by mankind
It's a crime of betrayal
of abandonment
of deception
of subjugation
of deception
of deprivation
It is a crime of the robbery of my childhood
by sweet devilish uncles who generously replaced it
With motherhood.

My monstrous uncles had to send me off
to join the 11 trailered passenger train of the
Filthy rich grey bearded 77 year old Zvandada
So that my widowed mother can feed from my dowry,
But all she got was a basket of maize and a starving goat
Whose visible myriad of ribs are a menace to the hungry owner.

When a playground is replaced with a kitchen
Life becomes a terrifying nightmare.
The hardship of memorising the 3 times table
was far much better
than memorising the recipe of a husband's favourite dish.

No more enjoying mom's sweet lullabies
Now enduring the suffocating the drunken breath.
The breath that strangled my innocence
The breath that burnt my premature dreams
without producing a warming heat nor ashes
But only this dark soot!

Oh the just one!
Wipe away the sour tears of this poor 12 year old
Twelfth wife of Zvandada
Who can no longer feed the tick that has sucked
All the life out of her.
The poor wife whose widowed mother starved to death
And buried in a golden casket by her generous uncles
And was lashed by her husband because of her unfortunate
miscarriage.
Labelled a generation disgracer by the 11 senior wives!
"Mbudzi kuzvarirawo pavanhu hunzi nditandirwe imbwa"
Oh Justice Trust Munatsi hear my plea!

For your just judgement is like rain that falls on an exhausted
Kalahari traveller
It revives a thousand souls of married girl children
And is dawn that liberates the girl child from the bondage of early
motherhood.
It is high time we put an end to daylight robbery of childhood from
the Zimbabwean girl!

Publisher's List

If you have enjoyed *Ghetto Symphony*, consider these other fine books from Mwanaka Media and Publishing:

Cultural Hybridity and Fixity by Andrew Nyongesa
The Water Cycle by Andrew Nyongesa
Tintinnabulation of Literary Theory by Andrew Nyongesa
I Threw a Star in a Wine Glass by Fethi Sassi
South Africa and United Nations Peacekeeping Offensive Operations by Antonio Garcia
Africanization and Americanization Anthology Volume 1, Searching for Interracial, Interstitial, Intersectional and Interstates Meeting Spaces, Africa Vs North America by Tendai R Mwanaka
A Conversation..., A Contact by Tendai Rinos Mwanaka
A Dark Energy by Tendai Rinos Mwanaka
Africa, UK and Ireland: Writing Politics and Knowledge Production Vol 1 by Tendai R Mwanaka
Best New African Poets 2017 Anthology by Tendai R Mwanaka and Daniel Da Purificacao
Keys in the River: New and Collected Stories by Tendai Rinos Mwanaka
Logbook Written by a Drifter by Tendai Rinos Mwanaka
Mad Bob Republic: Bloodlines, Bile and Crying Child by Tendai Rinos Mwanaka
How The Twins Grew Up/Makurire Akaita Mapatya by Milutin Djurickovic and Tendai Rinos Mwanaka
Writing Language, Culture and Development, Africa Vs Asia Vol 1 by Tendai R Mwanaka, Wanjohi wa Makokha and Upal Deb
Zimbolicious Poetry Vol 1 by Tendai R Mwanaka and Edward Dzonze

Zimbolicious: An Anthology of Zimbabwean Literature and Arts, Vol 3 by Tendai Mwanaka

Under The Steel Yoke by Jabulani Mzinyathi

A Case of Love and Hate by Chenjerai Mhondera

Epochs of Morning Light by Elena Botts

Fly in a Beehive by Thato Tshukudu

Bounding for Light by Richard Mbuthia

White Man Walking by John Eppel

A Cat and Mouse Affair by Bruno Shora

Sentiments by Jackson Matimba

Best New African Poets 2018 Anthology by Tendai R Mwanaka and Nsah Mala

Drawing Without Licence by Tendai R Mwanaka

Writing Grandmothers/ Escribiendo sobre nuestras raíces: Africa Vs Latin America Vol 2 by Tendai R Mwanaka and Felix Rodriguez

The Scholarship Girl by Abigail George

Words That Matter by Gerry Sikazwe

The Gods Sleep Through It by Wonder Guchu

The Ungendered by Delia Watterson

The Big Noise and Other Noises by Christopher Kudyahakudadirwe

Tiny Human Protection Agency by Megan Landman

Soon to be released

Of Bloom Smoke by Abigail George

Sky for a Foreign Bird by Fethi Sassi

Denga reshiri yokunze kwenyika by Fethi Sassi

A Portrait of Defiance by Tendai Rinos Mwanaka

Nationalism: (Mis)Understanding   Donald Trump's Capitalism, Racism, Global Politics, International Trade and Media Wars, Africa Vs North America Vol 2 by Tendai R Mwanaka

Where I Belong: moments, mist and song by Smeetha Bhoumik

Ashes by Ken Weene and Umar O. Abdul

Ouafa and the Thawra: About a Lover From Tunisia by Arturo Desimone

Thoughts Hunt The Loves/Pfungwa dzinovhima Vadiwa by Jeton Kelmendi

When Escape Becomes the only Lover by Tendai R Mwanaka

https://facebook.com/MwanakaMediaAndPublishing/

61

Printed in the United States
By Bookmasters